Introduction

There is money to be made in the vending business. You most likely have a full time job and are trying to supplement your income. Or you are retired, maybe a student either way you can be successful in the bulk candy vending business.

Be careful when buying machines not to fall for the slick presentations and colorful graphics showing your estimated projected earnings. These projections rarely pan out as the vending business can vary greatly by location.

Be on the lookout for expense turnkey packages that want to sell you 10 machines at a time. Take your time and get your feet wet make sure the vending business is right for you before making such a large investment.

These companies try to sell you some magic secret about the vending business and the secret is there isn't one. You have to work hard to find the right locations and work to keep the accounts filled and the customers happy. Not quick and you won't be getting rich.

The other big factor is how much the machines cost you. Obviously a $50 machine is profitable much faster than a $150 machine.

I would suggest always buying used machines using craigslist or a similar website to source machines.

Many people fall for the glossy sales packages only to find they don't like the business and their soon ready to sell off their machines cheap just to be rid of them.

You can make money in the bulk candy vending business but it takes hard work good locations, quality machines and great service.

Business Plan

Setting goals and doing the math.

It's important to always treat your vending machines like a business and like any business you need a plan and you need to do the math to make sure it works for you.

When placing bulk candy machines it's very important to have a good business plan because you place the machine and may have to wait 30 days to see if you've made a bad placement on location.

So good or bad it may be a month before you know how well your machine is doing so it's important to keep good accounting. Always know how much the machine cost you total including shipping cost and cost of the candy inside the machine.

Your business plan needs to include machine maintenance cost, buying bulk products, accounting, and route building expenses. Your profit will take place over many days through many small transactions 25 cents at a time, so keep an eye on every quarter.

A business plan helps you set goals for acquiring new locations for your route and it also helps you set minimum amounts that each location should produce for you to leave the machines at that location.

The business plan needs to have goals that you wanting to achieve in the long and short term. You need to consider some basic things including.

How much time can you devote to your vending business?

Are you wanting a long term business or building a route to sell?

If your business grows are you comfortable hiring employees?

Do you have to money to start a vending machine business?

Do you have space for extra machine parts and candy stocks?

Are you an entrepreneur?

You need to realistically think about these questions a vending machine business can be profitable but like any business there is work involved. It takes time out your day to fill the machines and also to buy the candy and do maintenance it's a real commitment.

Vending machines have a lot of upfront cost so it's important to keep good numbers so you know at what point your machines break even and when they go into profit.

Looking at those numbers can also help you decide between buying new or used machines.

Depending on how much you paid for the machine and how busy the location is it could take months or over a year to be profitable with a bulk candy vending machine.

Bulk candy vending is not a quick rich quick scheme but you can get into profits much faster by watching closely the money coming in and the money going out.

Part of your business plan will include how you plan to grow your business. You can grow slowly adding one machine at a time and placing it yourself or you can buy many machines at once and hire a company to place them all for you. You can also buy someone else's route they have already built up.

Unlike one big business like a store your vending machine business is spread out over many locations you will have to keep good records of where the machines are located and who your contact person is at that location.

Good records are necessary for building your route you need to know what types of businesses are most profitable for you and you want to keep your route relatively close to each other to cut down servicing time.

The larger you can grow your route the more you can take advantage of bulk candy pricing generally the more you buy of a product the cheaper it becomes.

Failure to create even a simple business plan can result in unnecessary headaches and a painful loss of profits.

The cost of running any small business is a huge factor and vending machines are no different if you don't have a firm grasp of your number you don't really know if you are making money or not.

Commission or Charity?

How charity vending works

As vending machine operators you contact a charity that has a vendor outreach program. The cost is nominal generally one dollar per machine a month paid yearly, so $12 a year given to the charity.

The idea when placing the machine on location is to make the store owner feel like you are connected with the charity and are making on going monthly contributions that are a percentage of what the machine takes in. That is false.

Many vendor route operators justify the small amount paid to the charities by correctly stating the charities set up the program and the pricing, so it's legitimate.

I have never felt completely comfortable with the charity model and have never been an advocate of it.

How commission vending works

Setting up your vending route through commission is better. You are approaching small business owners not begging for a questionable charity but with a simple business proposition.

The business has a little unused space and customer flow. Your product does not compete with what the store sells and their customers will benefit from the vending machine.

Start with 10% and negotiate to 30% or higher depending on how valuable you think the location could be.

Any large location is going to require you pay them at least 30% of the profits before your expenses. Smaller locations will do a charity machine because they are smaller locations and you are more likely to be talking to the owner.

The charity vending route is largely why vending operators have received a bad reputation. People often feel like the stickers are a scam and to be honest they largely are.

Best Selling Candies

Selling the right bulk candy is important generally you will only check your machines once a month so a poor selling candy can really hurt profits. Each of your locations will be different so monitor what candy works in which location.

You can make a small flier that informs the business owner of the candies that you can provide in the machine and allow them to pick. Or you can simply go with your best sellers from other locations and monitor the new location. Making a list of available candies stops the business owner from asking you to vend something you can't supply.

You may find in your area that there are items that sell really well at one location but not so well at another. Below is a good starter list of candies to begin they are top sellers nationally.

Peanut M&M's	Plain M&M's	Skittles
Reese's Pieces	Mike & Ikes	Gumballs
Hot Tamales	Runts	Baked Beans
Cashews	Peanuts	Trail Mix

Keep in mind cashews and peanuts will make more of a mess than skittles or gumballs and may not be worth the effort. Try to stock your machine with a variety when possible.

If you have 3 or more heads on your machine stock Sweet, Salty, and Sour to give the most variety. If you have a single head machine gumballs will give the highest profit margin but chocolate will sale the quickest.

It's up to you to monitor each machine and treat each location as its own market place keeping it stocked with the candy that sells best there.

Even if you get a really good deal on some candy for your machines if it's an untested brand you increase your risk of having a flop candy and losing profits.

Controlling Cost

Buying in bulk and reducing spoilage are the only controls you have over cost. Searching online and in your local stores for the absolute best price is crucial.

Bulk vending is a business that comes down to pennies and it's important to never over pay and always look for discounts. If you're buying locally look for sale days and coupons. Use redemption points to save more money.

Don't assume that online prices will beat local store prices with bulk candy the added shipping cost can easily make online options more expensive.

Eliminating spoilage is a matter of keeping good records and knowing what items sell at which locations. Harder bulk candies like skittles and runts will have the longest shelf life while chocolate coated candies and nuts will have a shorter life.

Nuts or trail mix are especially fragile and can actually mold inside the vending machine is not vended within a few weeks while skittles will stay stable for months.

You can eliminate spoilage by vending capsules out of your machine. You need a specific wheel to vend 1" or 2" capsules but the added cost of changing wheels is often made up with the added profits made from lack of spoilage.

You won't find capsules locally but a quick google search returns several distributors.

Finding Locations

Location is the biggest part of almost every business and vending is no different.

A three headed machine placed in a good location may return $30 a month in sales. In a great location it may do $50 a month in a poor location the same machine may do $8 a month or it may do nothing.

The best locations are the most obvious. You need lots of people and it doesn't matter if they are employees of a business or customers. It only matters that there are people on location and the machine is visible.

You will know within the first month or two how profitable the machine will be. Unless the machine is in a tourist area your monthly should not vary much.

Placing machines in large locations like Walmart and dollar generals is almost going to impossible as you are first starting out.

It makes more sense to focus on smaller locations where the owner or decision maker for the business is likely to be on site.

Be prepared to offer a commission to be in the business generally between 10%-30% is acceptable and some business owners will want rent paid to place the machine generally $10 for a small machine per month. You have to monitor the location and judge for yourself if it's worth it.

Finding the right person to talk to if often the hardest part, small business owners are often busy people and it may take some time to get a face to face with a decision maker.

What's a good location? You name it as long as there's a consistent flow of traffic there is potential for profit at that location. No location is guaranteed profits but finding places with lots of foot traffic increases your odds a lot.

Try getting your machines placed close to the front door or at some locations close to the cash register remind the business owner that having a vending machine on location is a service for his/her customers.

If you enter a location and there is already a machine on location don't be afraid to ask to place your machine still. America was built on competition and it's good for everyone.

Provide a better, faster, cleaner service than your competition and you will do just fine.

Growth and Building

Adding new locations to your already existing route is a great way to grow your business. A less used idea is to increase your foot print in current locations.

A good idea is to monitor your locations placing a single head at each site and seeing how they do. After a few months a few locations may require a double or triple headed machine or a five head rack.

 If you are paying the location a commission they generally won't mind an increase in equipment as it leads to their increased profit.

It's easier to work with a business you already have a relationship with. Also the owner at some point may ask you to expand and add new machines.

Monitor your locations well and keep the owners happy. The business owners at your locations know other business owners so don't be afraid to ask for referrals to other business owners that may need vending.

Inventory

Inventory needs to be kept track of to insure profits and to make sure money is available to try new products. Keep track of both bestselling, and worst selling snacks. Also noting expiration dates for candy rotation.

Cost, space and availability all play into what you need in your inventory as do the number of machines in your route. Ordering often and keeping in stock your best sellers at all times.

Overtime you will recognize what the customers at each location prefer. No matter how good your best seller does you always to keep experimenting with new snacks.

This is one of the reasons I prefer a two headed machine as you can keep a best seller in one head and experiment with the other.

Keep in mind there are seasonal snacks that will sell well also there's regional snack favorites. Keep your untested snacks to low levels though, never buy a lot at one time even at a great price. Bulk candy has a long expiration time but it does expire.

Make sure if you order your inventory online you keep a few weeks inventory on hand. If you get it locally there's no real need.

When ordering look for seasonal changes if there are any. Ideally your inventory runs out as your new inventory comes in so you don't have a lot of inventory on hand.

 You can do this by keeping good track of how much your machines do on average and ordering accordingly. Keep seasonal weather changes in mind when ordering.

The middle of summer might not be the best time to have Reese's pieces outside in you vending machine or sitting in your inventory.

Storage

You will need a dedicated area to store your bulk candy. Even if you only have one machine you need to take this part seriously as you are storing edibles.

Contact the officials in your to get a certification if that's necessary to handle food in vending machines in your area. You are responsible for complying with local laws and ordinances.

Snacks for bulk candy machines can generally be stored on a shelf in a clean dry area. If you have just a few machines you can simply donate a shelf in a kitchen cabinet to your vending business.

If you are buying candy locally you can grow your business quite large without needing much storage. If you are ordering products online you will need more space but a small closet can hold enough bulk supplies to fill well over fifty machines so for most people storage will not be an issue.

How Valuable is That Location?

Is your location valuable? Keeping good records will help you to determine the value of your locations.

Add up the amount of money the machine makes in a 30 day period minus expenses, cost of candy etc. and that is the actual net dollar amount the location makes for you but it's not necessarily the value.

It also matters how easy the account is to service how close it to your home and various other things can play in the true value of a location.

Taking into account all your expenses including time and gas a location that makes a little less money but is closer to your home may be a more valuable location to you then one that makes a little more money all the way across town.

You can figure out when your vending machine is in profits by looking at your monthly numbers. Let's do a quick example using a placement service.

Used bulk candy machine from craigslist = $50

Candy to put in the machine = $20

Placement service cost = $50

Total to place a full candy machine = $120

Average monthly income after expenses = $15

With this example you are profitable in *8 months*.

Not using a placement service you are profitable in 4 and half months.

$15 a month doesn't seem like much but it's the real national average. If you have several machines on location you will learn that estimates of $50 a month per machine are highly inflated.

Look at your numbers often to identify your best locations and don't be afraid to pull a machine from a slow location.

You only have a certain amount of machines to place and a set amount of time to service them so make sure you are focusing on the most profitable locations on your route.

Placing or Locating Machines

There are two ways to get your vending machines on location you will need to go into the business and ask to place the machine or you will have to hire a company that will cold call locations and try to place the machines for you. Both ways can work.

If you plan on placing the machines yourself it would really help to be a good salesperson with a lot of local business owners as friends around town. If not and you want to place machines yourself you will want to get a script written that you can use when talking to potential locations.

You will want to introduce yourself tell the owner or manager about your service and ask to place the machine at their location.

Be prepared to hear NO it is going to happen. You will have owners tell you that've had vending machines before and they didn't make money or they were too messy.

This is where you will have to be a sales person and assure them that the financial risk is all on your side and you will do a good job servicing the machines.

Working with a local charity can also be a good way of getting business owners to let you place the machines and can be a great way to help a small local charity.

You don't have to walk into a business you can also cold call locations and ask to speak to the manager if you are comfortable talking on the phone. You can call far more places than you can walk into in a day.

If you are a regular customer at a local restaurant or small thrift store don't be afraid to ask to leave your machine in the location all they can say is no.

Don't forget to ask friends and family they don't have to be business owners themselves but as employees they can let you know the vending situation at their work places.

You can also hire a placement service to locate a business to place your vending machine. The service is currently about $52 for a single head machine.

At any given time you will find 3-4 large vending machine locators available and a few smaller ones. They tend to go in and out of favor you success with these companies will vary.

Vending machine placement companies basically cold call locations in your area to find you leads. The good companies will check number of employees of the business and size location to make sure you get a nice location.

Often the locating company will simply put your area code in there system and start cold calling every number in your area.

Locating services will include a warranty that states that if you lose the location in 30 or less they will replace it. You may also find companies that will guarantee a certain amount of revenue or they will replace the machine locations.

You have to check each service and find the one best suited to your needs.

Lastly, you shouldn't ever pay the full amount until after you get your locations. Good locators will need 50% up front typically which is ok as long as you screen them well.

Paying 100% up front is asking too much in my opinion unless you have worked with them in the past or they have raving reviews.

Be a Good Vendor

It's hard to get good locations so it's important to keep them. Doing these ten things consistently will help you to keep locations longer

Free Candy. If the manager or some employees are around when you refill the machines give them each a quarter and let them get a snack. It will promote good will with the business.

Be Nice. When you enter into a business be smiling you are a professional and should be greeting customers and employees of the business with respect.

Be Clean. Dirty machines will certainly make less money than clean ones. You want the business to look at your machines a service to their customers not an eyesore they have to clean up after.

Restock Often. Keeping fresh products in your machines is important you never want someone complaining to management that the candy machine has stale product.

Don't Sell Out. You never want an empty slot of a popular product. If you find certain products sell very well consider double stocking that candy in the machine.

Ask Somebody. Ask the employees how they like having the machine on location you may learn some valuable information that helps to keep the location longer.

Give Value. Don't expect a machine filled with the cheapest candy available to get used very often. People want value even in vending and offering the top brands really will increase sales.

Don't Break. Machines malfunction it happens but if you keep having a machine break downs at a location you may lose that location. Anytime a machine breaks at a location replace that machine entirely.

Be Relevant. Think of your location, you clients your region etc. when stocking your machines. Give the people the candy they want not necessarily the candy you can get the best price on.

Look Nice. You don't need a suit put you should look clean and professional when you enter a business. You are a reflection of your business keeping yourself nice and your machines nice will help you keep locations

Ultimately you want to build relationships with the business where you place your vending machines you can do that by following the steps above.

www.ingramcontent.com/pod-product-compliance
Lightning Source LLC
Chambersburg PA
CBHW050039230526
45470CB00003B/1356